Contents

20

32

60

30

Kid
Favorites

SIMPLE DESSERTS KIDS LOVE

PREP TIME: 20 MINUTES

OREO frogs

2	squares **BAKER'S** Semi-Sweet Chocolate
2	Tbsp. butter or margarine
12	**OREO** Cookies
1/4	cup **JET-PUFFED** Marshmallow Creme
24	miniature pretzel twists
24	candy-coated chocolate pieces

MICROWAVE chocolate and butter in microwaveable bowl on HIGH 1 min. or until chocolate is completely melted and mixture is well blended, stirring every 30 sec.

SPREAD bottom of each cookie with 1 tsp. marshmallow creme, then dip bottom in melted chocolate. Immediately press 2 pretzel twists into chocolate for each frog's legs, with wide part of each pretzel facing outward. Place, pretzel-sides down, on waxed paper-covered baking sheet.

USE remaining melted chocolate to attach candies to tops of cookies for frog's eyes. Let stand until chocolate is firm.

MAKES: 6 servings.

substitute:
Substitute peanut butter for the marshmallow creme.

Nutrition Information Per Serving: 240 calories, 12g total fat, 6g saturated fat, 270mg sodium, 32g carbohydrate, 18g sugars, 2g protein.

OREO-apple snack stacks

1 pkg. (8 oz.) **PHILADELPHIA** Cream Cheese, softened

2 Tbsp. honey

1/2 tsp. zest and 2 Tbsp. juice from 1 orange, divided

6 **OREO** Cookies, chopped

4 small apples (1 lb.)

4 pretzel sticks

8 worm-shaped chewy fruit snacks

MIX cream cheese, honey and zest in medium bowl until well blended. Stir in chopped cookies. Core apples. Cut each crosswise into 4 rings; brush cut sides with orange juice. Discard any remaining juice.

PAT apple slices dry with paper towels; spread with cream cheese mixture. Restack slices for each apple. Insert pretzel into top of each for the stem.

GARNISH with fruit snacks. Cut horizontally in half to serve.

MAKES: 8 servings.

make ahead:
Snacks can be made ahead of time. Prepare as directed; wrap with plastic wrap. Refrigerate until ready to serve.

Nutrition Information Per Serving: 210 calories, 11g total fat, 6g saturated fat, 170mg sodium, 25g carbohydrate, 19g sugars, 3g protein.

OREO milk shake

    4   tsp. chocolate syrup

    8   **OREO** Cookies, divided

1½   cups milk

    2   cups **BREYERS**® All Natural Vanilla Ice Cream, softened

SPOON 1 tsp. syrup into each of 4 glasses. Roll each glass to coat bottom and inside of glass. Finely chop 4 cookies; set aside.

QUARTER remaining cookies; place in blender. Add milk and ice cream; blend until smooth.

POUR into prepared glasses; top with chopped cookies. Serve immediately.

MAKES: 4 servings, about 1 cup each.

BREYERS is a registered trademark of Unilever Group of Companies. © Unilever.

substitute:

For a lower calorie and fat option, use Reduced Fat OREO and BREYERS® Smooth & Dreamy™ Fat-Free Vanilla Ice Cream.

Nutrition Information Per Serving: 300 calories, 13g total fat, 7g saturated fat, 220mg sodium, 40g carbohydrate, 32g sugars, 6g protein.

dirt cups

  1 pkg. (3.9 oz.) **JELL-O** Chocolate Instant Pudding

  2 cups cold milk

  1 tub (8 oz.) **COOL WHIP** Whipped Topping, thawed

15 **OREO** Cookies, finely crushed (about 1 1/4 cups), divided

10 worm-shaped chewy fruit snacks

BEAT pudding mix and milk in large bowl with whisk 2 min. Let stand 5 min. Stir in **COOL WHIP** and 1/2 cup cookie crumbs.

SPOON into 10 (6- to 7-oz.) paper or plastic cups; top with remaining cookie crumbs.

REFRIGERATE 1 hour. Top with fruit snacks just before serving.

MAKES: 10 servings.

sand cups: ◄

Prepare using JELL-O Vanilla Flavor Instant Pudding and 35 NILLA Wafers.

Nutrition Information Per Serving: 230 calories, 9g total fat, 6g saturated fat, 290mg sodium, 36g carbohydrate, 24g sugars, 3g protein.

martians-ate-my-OREO cupcakes

1	pkg. (2-layer size) chocolate cake mix
1	pkg. (8 oz.) **PHILADELPHIA** Cream Cheese, softened
1	egg
2	Tbsp. sugar
54	Mini **OREO** Cookies, divided
2	or 3 drops green food coloring
2	cups thawed **COOL WHIP** Whipped Topping
4	**OREO** Cookies
¼	cup **JET-PUFFED** Miniature Marshmallows
4	**JET-PUFFED** Marshmallows, cut in half
2	pieces string licorice
1	Tbsp. assorted round candies

HEAT oven to 350°F.

PREPARE cake batter as directed on package. Mix cream cheese, egg and sugar until well blended. Spoon half the cake batter into 24 paper-lined muffin cups. Top each with about 2 tsp. cream cheese mixture and 1 mini cookie; cover with remaining batter.

BAKE 19 to 22 min. or until toothpick inserted in centers comes out clean. Cool 5 min.; remove from pans to wire racks. Cool completely.

STIR green food coloring into **COOL WHIP**; spread onto cupcakes. Split remaining mini and regular-size cookies, leaving all the filling on half of each cookie. Use with remaining ingredients to decorate cupcakes to resemble martians as shown in photo.

MAKES: 2 doz. or 24 servings.

Nutrition Information Per Serving: 250 calories, 15g total fat, 5g saturated fat, 280mg sodium, 28g carbohydrate, 17g sugars, 4g protein.

OREO baseball dessert

  1 pkg. (3.9 oz.) **JELL-O** Chocolate Instant Pudding

  2 cups cold milk

35 **OREO** Cookies, divided

1¹/₂ cups thawed **COOL WHIP** Whipped Topping

  1 piece red string licorice (36 inch)

BEAT pudding mix and milk with whisk 2 min. Let stand 5 min. or until thickened.

LINE 8-inch round pan with plastic wrap. Arrange 14 cookies on bottom of pan, cutting to fit if necessary; cover with 1 cup pudding. Repeat layers. Cover with plastic wrap. Refrigerate 24 hours.

UNCOVER dessert. Invert onto serving plate; remove plastic wrap. Frost dessert with **COOL WHIP**. Cut remaining cookies in half; arrange around edge of dessert. Cut licorice into 2 (8-inch) pieces and 20 (1-inch) pieces. Use licorice to decorate top of dessert to resemble a baseball.

MAKES: 10 servings.

how to easily cut cookies in half:

Refrigerate OREO Cookies first for about 15 min. Then, use a serrated knife to cut in half.

Nutrition Information Per Serving: 280 calories, 11g total fat, 5g saturated fat, 400mg sodium, 44g carbohydrate, 27g sugars, 4g protein.

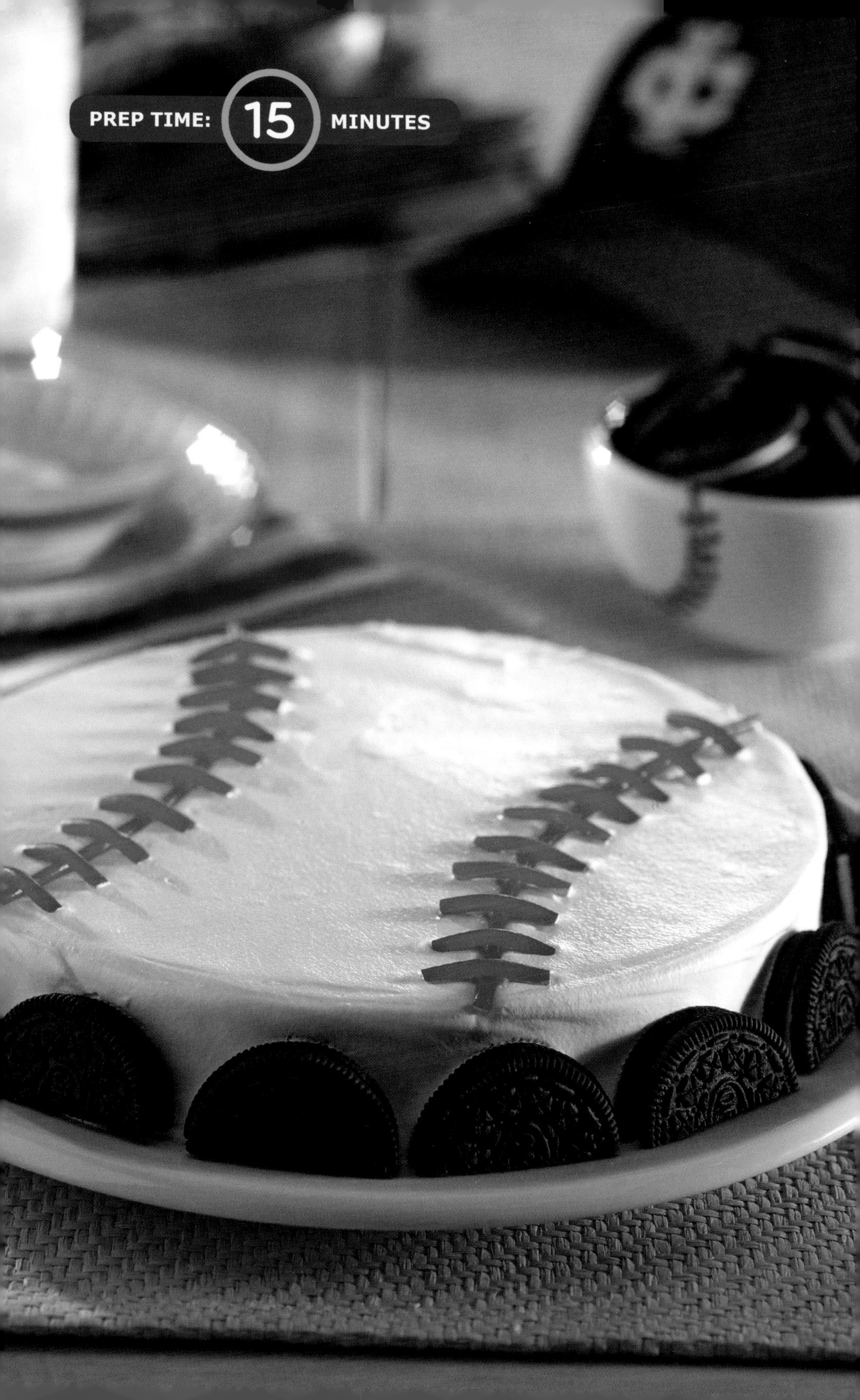
PREP TIME: 15 MINUTES

Frozen Treats

FROSTY DELIGHTS THAT PLEASE THE WHOLE FAMILY

PREP TIME: 20 MINUTES

NILLA tortoni "cake"

- 1 pkg. (12 oz.) **NILLA** Wafers (about 88 wafers), coarsely crushed (about 5 cups)
- 1 cup **PLANTERS** Slivered Almonds, toasted
- 1¾ qt. (7 cups) vanilla ice cream, softened
- ½ cup caramel ice cream topping

SPRINKLE 1 cup wafer crumbs and ⅓ cup nuts onto bottom of 9-inch springform pan; cover with half the ice cream. Repeat layers. Top with remaining crumbs and nuts; press into ice cream with back of spoon to secure.

FREEZE 4 hours.

REMOVE side of pan before cutting dessert into wedges to serve. Drizzle with caramel topping.

MAKES: *16 servings.*

▶ how to toast nuts:

Spread nuts into single layer in shallow pan. Bake at 350°F for 5 to 7 min. or until lightly toasted, stirring occasionally.

Nutrition Information Per Serving: 280 calories, 14g total fat, 5g saturated fat, 150mg sodium, 37g carbohydrate, 25g sugars, 5g protein.

OREO & fudge ice cream cake

$^1/_2$ cup hot fudge ice cream topping, warmed

1 tub (8 oz.) **COOL WHIP** Whipped Topping, thawed, divided

1 pkg. (3.9 oz.) **JELL-O** Chocolate Instant Pudding

16 **OREO** Cookies, chopped (about 2 cups), divided

12 vanilla ice cream sandwiches

POUR fudge topping into medium bowl. Whisk in 1 cup **COOL WHIP**. Add dry pudding mix; stir 2 min. Stir in 1 cup chopped cookies.

ARRANGE 4 ice cream sandwiches, side-by-side, on 24-inch-long piece of foil; top with half the **COOL WHIP** mixture. Repeat layers. Top with remaining sandwiches. Frost top and sides with remaining **COOL WHIP**; press remaining chopped cookies into **COOL WHIP** on top and sides of cake. Bring up foil sides; double fold top and ends to loosely seal packet.

FREEZE 4 hours.

MAKES: 12 servings.

note:
The consistency of fudge topping can vary depending on what brand you purchase. If your fudge topping mixture is too thick to spread easily, stir in up to $^1/_4$ cup milk.

Nutrition Information Per Serving: 370 calories, 15g total fat, 9g saturated fat, 410mg sodium, 56g carbohydrate, 32g sugars, 4g protein.

CHIPS AHOY! wiches

3   cups vanilla ice cream, slightly softened

24   **CHIPS AHOY!** Cookies

3/4   cup sprinkles

SPREAD 1/4 cup ice cream onto flat side of each of 12 cookies. Cover with remaining cookies to make 12 sandwiches.

ROLL edges in sprinkles.

FREEZE 1 to 2 hours or until firm.

MAKES: 1 doz. or 12 servings.

variation:

Prepare using your favorite flavor of ice cream, sherbet or frozen yogurt. In addition, roll edges in chopped PLANTERS Nuts, colored sprinkles, chocolate chips or toasted BAKER'S ANGEL FLAKE Coconut instead of the sprinkles.

Nutrition Information Per Serving: 220 calories, 9g total fat, 4g saturated fat, 105mg sodium, 35g carbohydrate, 26g sugars, 2g protein.

cherry-vanilla ice cream pie

18 **OREO** Cookies, finely crushed (about 1^1/$_2$ cups)

3 Tbsp. butter or margarine, melted

3 cups vanilla ice cream, softened

1 can (21 oz.) cherry pie filling, divided

1 Tbsp. chocolate syrup

COMBINE cookie crumbs and butter; press onto bottom and up side of 9-inch pie plate sprayed with cooking spray. Refrigerate until ready to use.

MIX ice cream and 1^1/$_2$ cups pie filling; spoon into crust. Freeze 4 hours or until firm.

DRIZZLE chocolate syrup over pie. Serve topped with remaining cherry pie filling.

MAKES: 10 servings.

substitute:
Prepare using a chocolate syrup that hardens to form a "shell" when drizzled over the pie.

Nutrition Information Per Serving: 280 calories, 12g total fat, 6g saturated fat, 180mg sodium, 41g carbohydrate, 30g sugars, 3g protein.

CHIPS AHOY! ice cream cake

1 pkg. (15.25 oz.) **CHIPS AHOY!** Cookies (39 cookies), divided

1/4 cup butter or margarine, melted

3/4 cup hot fudge ice cream topping, divided

3 cups vanilla ice cream, divided

3 cups chocolate ice cream, divided

3/4 cup thawed **COOL WHIP** Whipped Topping

7 maraschino cherries

SET aside 12 cookies. Crush remaining cookies; mix with butter. Press 2/3 onto bottom of 9-inch springform pan. Stand reserved cookies around edge. Microwave 1/2 cup fudge topping as directed on package; drizzle over crust. Freeze 15 min.

SOFTEN 1 1/2 cups of <u>each</u> flavor ice cream; spread, 1 flavor at a time, over fudge layer in crust. Sprinkle with remaining crumb mixture. Scoop remaining ice cream into balls; place over crumb layer.

FREEZE 4 hours or until firm. When ready to serve, top dessert with **COOL WHIP**. Microwave remaining fudge topping as directed on package; drizzle over dessert. Garnish with cherries.

MAKES: 12 servings.

note: If you don't have a springform pan, you can prepare dessert in 9-inch pie plate instead.

Nutrition Information Per Serving: 440 calories, 23g total fat, 11g saturated fat, 260mg sodium, 56g carbohydrate, 36g sugars, 5g protein.

OREO cookies & creme pudding pops

1 pkg. (3.4 oz.) **JELL-O** Vanilla Flavor Instant Pudding

2 cups cold milk

12 **OREO** Cookies, divided

1/2 cup thawed **COOL WHIP** Whipped Topping

BEAT pudding mix and milk in medium bowl with whisk 2 min.

CHOP 6 cookies; crush remaining cookies. Spoon half the crushed cookies onto bottoms of 10 (3-oz.) paper or plastic cups.

ADD chopped cookies and **COOL WHIP** to pudding; stir just until blended.

SPOON pudding mixture into cups; top with remaining crushed cookies. Insert wooden pop stick or plastic spoon into each for handle. Freeze 5 hours or until firm.

MAKES: 10 servings.

how to remove frozen pops from cups: ◄

Hold frozen cups with hands on sides of cups to warm pops slightly before removing from cups. To remove pops, press firmly onto bottom of cup to release pop. Do not twist or pull pop stick.

Nutrition Information Per Serving: 130 calories, 4.5g total fat, 2g saturated fat, 230mg sodium, 22g carbohydrate, 16g sugars, 2g protein.

frozen OREO fudge-pop squares

- 5 squares **BAKER'S** Semi-Sweet Chocolate, divided
- 18 **OREO** Cookies, crushed (about 1²/₃ cups)
- 3 Tbsp. butter or margarine, melted
- 2 tubs (8 oz. each) **PHILADELPHIA** Cream Cheese Spread
- 1 can (14 oz.) sweetened condensed milk
- 1 cup thawed **COOL WHIP** Whipped Topping

LINE 9-inch square pan with foil, with ends of foil extending over sides. Melt 4 chocolate squares as directed on package; set aside. Mix cookie crumbs and butter; press onto bottom of prepared pan.

BEAT cream cheese spread in large bowl with mixer until creamy. Gradually beat in milk. Blend in melted chocolate. Whisk in **COOL WHIP**. Spoon over crust. Freeze 6 hours. Meanwhile, make curls from remaining chocolate square.

REMOVE dessert from freezer 15 min. before serving. Top with chocolate curls. Use foil handles to lift dessert from pan.

MAKES: 16 servings.

how to make chocolate curls:

Warm a square of BAKER'S Baking Chocolate by microwaving it, unwrapped, on HIGH for a few seconds or just until you can smudge the chocolate with your thumb. Hold the square steadily and draw a peeler slowly over flat bottom of square, allowing a thin layer of chocolate to curl as it is peeled off the bottom of the square to make long, delicate curls. Use the same technique along the narrow side of the square to make short curls.

Nutrition Information Per Serving: 290 calories, 18g total fat, 11g saturated fat, 240mg sodium, 30g carbohydrate, 25g sugars, 4g protein.

Goodies To Go

CANDIES, MUFFINS, AND OTHER TREATS THAT ARE READY TO TRAVEL

PREP TIME: 20 MINUTES

CHIPS AHOY! turtles

 3 squares **BAKER'S** Semi-Sweet Chocolate, divided
 1 Tbsp. butter or margarine
12 **CHIPS AHOY!** Cookies
 6 **KRAFT** Caramels
 2 tsp. milk
12 **PLANTERS** Pecan Halves

MICROWAVE 2 chocolate squares and butter in microwaveable bowl on HIGH 1 min. or until chocolate is melted and mixture is well blended, stirring every 30 sec. Spread onto tops of cookies. Let stand 15 min. or until chocolate is firm.

MICROWAVE caramels and milk in small microwaveable bowl on HIGH 1 min.; stir until smooth. Melt remaining chocolate square as directed on package.

SPOON caramel onto centers of cookies; top with nuts. Drizzle with melted chocolate. Let stand 30 min.

MAKES: 1 doz. or 12 servings.

gift-giving:
To give as a gift, pack several cookie turtles in decorative container or tin lined with colorful plastic wrap or tissue paper.

Nutrition Information Per Serving: 120 calories, 7g total fat, 3g saturated fat, 60mg sodium, 15g carbohydrate, 9g sugars, 1g protein.

OREO chocolate-raspberry truffle cups

¹/₄ cup butter or margarine, divided

12 **OREO** Cookies, finely crushed (about 1 cup)

2 Tbsp. raspberry jam

1 pkg. (6 squares) **BAKER'S** White Chocolate

¹/₂ cup whipping cream, divided

6 squares **BAKER'S** Semi-Sweet Chocolate

2 Tbsp. white or multi-colored sprinkles

MELT 2 Tbsp. butter; mix with cookie crumbs. Press onto bottoms of 24 miniature paper-lined muffin cups. Add ¹/₄ tsp. jam to each. Refrigerate until ready to use.

MICROWAVE white chocolate, ¹/₄ cup cream and 1 Tbsp. of the remaining butter in microwaveable bowl on HIGH 1 min.; stir until chocolate is melted and mixture is well blended. Spoon over jam. Freeze 10 min.

MEANWHILE, melt semi-sweet chocolate with remaining cream and butter as directed for white chocolate. Spoon over white chocolate layer; top with sprinkles. Refrigerate 1 to 2 hours or until firm.

MAKES: 2 doz. or 24 servings.

substitute:

For variety, substitute marshmallow creme, peanut butter, caramel sauce or a different flavor of jam for the raspberry jam in the recipe.

Nutrition Information Per Serving: 140 calories, 9g total fat, 5g saturated fat, 50mg sodium, 15g carbohydrate, 12g sugars, 1g protein.

double-chocolate OREO fudge

   6 cups sugar, divided

1½ cups butter or margarine, divided

   2 small cans (5 oz. each) evaporated milk (about ⅔ cup each)

1½ pkg. (12 squares) **BAKER'S** Semi-Sweet Chocolate

   2 jars (7 oz. each) **JET-PUFFED** Marshmallow Creme, divided

   1 cup chopped **PLANTERS** Macadamias

   2 tsp. vanilla, divided

   2 pkg. (6 squares each) **BAKER'S** White Chocolate

   8 **OREO** Cookies, chopped

LINE 13×9-inch pan with foil, with ends of foil extending over sides. Place 3 cups sugar, ¾ cup butter and 1 can evaporated milk in 3-qt. heavy saucepan. Bring to full rolling boil on medium heat, stirring constantly. Cook 4 min. or until candy thermometer reaches 234°F, stirring constantly. Remove from heat.

ADD semi-sweet chocolate and 1 jar marshmallow creme; stir until melted. Add nuts and 1 tsp. vanilla; mix well. Pour into prepared pan; spread to cover bottom of pan.

BRING remaining sugar, butter and evaporated milk to full rolling boil in separate 3-qt. heavy saucepan on medium heat, stirring constantly. Cook 4 min. or until candy thermometer reaches 234°F, stirring constantly. Remove from heat.

ADD white chocolate and remaining marshmallow creme; stir until melted. Stir in chopped cookies and remaining vanilla. Pour over chocolate layer in pan; spread to evenly cover. Cool at room temperature 4 hours before cutting into pieces. Store in tightly covered container at room temperature.

MAKES: 6¼ lb. or 72 servings, 1 piece each.

cooking know-how:

If you don't have a candy thermometer, bring sugar mixture to full rolling boil on medium heat, then begin timing 4 min. while mixture continues to boil, stirring constantly.

Nutrition Information Per Serving: 190 calories, 9g total fat, 4.5g saturated fat, 50mg sodium, 28g carbohydrate, 26g sugars, 1g protein.

easy OREO truffles

1 pkg. (8 oz.) **PHILADELPHIA** Cream Cheese, softened

1 pkg. (1 lb. 2 oz.) **OREO** Cookies, finely crushed (about 4¼ cups), divided

2 pkg. (8 squares each) **BAKER'S** Semi-Sweet Chocolate, melted

MIX cream cheese and 3 cups cookie crumbs until well blended.

SHAPE into 48 (1-inch) balls. Dip in melted chocolate; place on waxed paper-covered baking sheet. Sprinkle with remaining cookie crumbs.

REFRIGERATE 1 hour or until firm.

MAKES: 4 doz. or 48 servings.

how to easily dip truffles: ◄ ------------------------

To easily coat truffles with the melted chocolate, add truffles, in batches, to bowl of melted chocolate. Use 2 forks to roll truffles in chocolate until evenly coated. Remove truffles with forks, letting excess chocolate drip back into bowl.

Nutrition Information Per Serving: 100 calories, 6g total fat, 3g saturated fat, 75mg sodium, 11g carbohydrate, 7g sugars, 1g protein.

CHIPS AHOY! bark

  1 pkg. (8 squares) **BAKER'S** Semi-Sweet Chocolate, chopped

  1 pkg. (6 squares) **BAKER'S** White Chocolate, chopped

10 **CHIPS AHOY!** Cookies, coarsely broken, divided

 1/4 cup dried cranberries, divided

MICROWAVE semi-sweet and white chocolates in separate medium microwaveable bowls as directed on package. Stir 1/3 cup cookies and 1 Tbsp. cranberries into chocolate in each bowl.

DROP spoonfuls of the 2 chocolate mixtures alternately onto waxed paper-covered baking sheet; swirl gently with knife. Sprinkle with remaining cookies and cranberries.

REFRIGERATE 1 hour or until firm. Break into pieces.

MAKES: 14 servings.

special extra: ◄---
Toast 1/4 cup PLANTERS Slivered Almonds. Add 1 Tbsp. nuts to melted chocolate in each bowl before dropping onto baking sheet and swirling as directed. Sprinkle with remaining nuts, cookies and cranberries.

Nutrition Information Per Serving: 190 calories, 11g total fat, 6g saturated fat, 35mg sodium, 24g carbohydrate, 19g sugars, 2g protein.

Sweet Celebrations

DESSERT CREATIONS
FOR ALL OCCASIONS

PREP TIME: 10 MINUTES

cookie "fun-due"

1 pkg. (8 squares) **BAKER'S** Semi-Sweet Chocolate
1 cup whipping cream
   CHIPS AHOY! Cookies

MICROWAVE chocolate and whipping cream in large microwaveable bowl on HIGH 2 min. or until chocolate is completely melted and mixture is well blended, stirring after each minute.

SERVE warm with **CHIPS AHOY!** Cookies for dipping.

MAKES: 1³/₄ cups or 14 servings, 2 Tbsp. dip and 3 cookies each.

special extra:

Serve with additional dippers, such as OREO Cookies, OREO CAKESTERS Soft Snack Cakes, NILLA Wafers, HONEY MAID Graham Crackers, JET-PUFFED Marshmallows, strawberries, banana chunks and apple slices.

Nutrition Information Per Serving: 290 calories, 19g total fat, 9g saturated fat, 120mg sodium, 32g carbohydrate, 18g sugars, 3g protein.

mini OREO cheesecakes

44	**OREO** Cookies, divided
3	pkg. (8 oz. each) **PHILADELPHIA** Cream Cheese, softened
3/4	cup sugar
3/4	cup **BREAKSTONE'S** or **KNUDSEN** Sour Cream
1	tsp. vanilla
3	eggs
2	squares **BAKER'S** White Chocolate, melted
1/2	cup colored sprinkles
1 1/2	cups thawed **COOL WHIP** Whipped Topping

HEAT oven to 325°F.

PLACE 1 cookie in each of 24 foil- or paper-lined muffin pan cups. Chop 8 of the remaining cookies; set aside.

BEAT cream cheese and sugar with mixer until blended. Add sour cream and vanilla; mix well. Add eggs, 1 at a time, beating after each just until blended. Gently stir in chopped cookies. Spoon into baking cups.

BAKE 18 to 20 min. or until centers are set. Cool completely. Refrigerate 3 hours or until chilled. Meanwhile, cut remaining cookies in half. Dip cookie halves halfway in melted chocolate. Place on waxed paper-covered baking sheet; top with sprinkles. Let stand 15 min. or until chocolate is firm.

TOP each cheesecake with dollop of **COOL WHIP** and cookie half just before serving.

MAKES: 2 doz. or 24 servings.

make ahead:
Cheesecakes can be stored in refrigerator up to 3 days, or frozen up to 1 month, before topping with COOL WHIP and cookie half just before serving. If freezing cheesecakes, thaw overnight in refrigerator before garnishing.

Nutrition Information Per Serving: 280 calories, 17g total fat, 9g saturated fat, 230mg sodium, 29g carbohydrate, 21g sugars, 4g protein.

chocolate-caramel creme pie

- 4   oz. (1/2 of 8-oz. pkg.) **PHILADELPHIA** Cream Cheese, softened
- 2   Tbsp. caramel ice cream topping
- 1   cup thawed **COOL WHIP** Whipped Topping
- 1   **OREO** Pie Crust (recipe follows)
- 1   pkg. (3.9 oz.) **JELL-O** Chocolate Instant Pudding
- 1½ cups cold milk

MIX cream cheese and caramel topping in medium bowl until well blended. Gently stir in **COOL WHIP**; spread onto bottom of **OREO** Pie Crust.

BEAT pudding mix and milk with whisk 2 min.; pour over cream cheese layer. Refrigerate 3 hours.

MAKES: 8 servings.

Nutrition Information Per Serving: 310 calories, 17g total fat, 10g saturated fat, 460mg sodium, 38g carbohydrate, 25g sugars, 4g protein.

OREO PIE CRUST

PREP: 15 min. TOTAL: 15 min.

- 18   **OREO** Cookies
- 3   Tbsp. butter or margarine, melted

PLACE cookies in large resealable plastic bag; press bag to remove excess air, then seal bag. Use rolling pin to crush cookies to form fine crumbs.

ADD butter; squeeze bag to evenly moisten crumbs.

PRESS crumb mixture onto bottom and up side of 9-inch pie plate sprayed with cooking spray. Refrigerate until ready to fill.

MAKES: 1 (9-inch) crust, 8 servings.

Nutrition Information Per Serving: 150 calories, 9g total fat, 4.5g saturated fat, 160mg sodium, 18g carbohydrate, 10g sugars, 1g protein.

PREP TIME: 30 MINUTES

how to easily serve crumb crust pies:

When serving a crumb-crust pie, dip filled pie plate in warm water for 10 sec., being careful to dip pie plate to just below rim. This will help loosen the crust to make it easier to serve the cut pieces.

molten chocolate surprise

4 squares **BAKER'S** Semi-Sweet Chocolate

$1/2$ cup butter or margarine

2 whole eggs

2 egg yolks

1 cup powdered sugar

$1/3$ cup flour

12 **CHIPS AHOY!** Cookies

$1/2$ cup thawed **COOL WHIP** Whipped Topping

HEAT oven to 425°F.

MICROWAVE chocolate and butter in large microwaveable bowl on HIGH 2 min. or until butter is melted. Stir until chocolate is completely melted. Beat whole eggs, yolks, sugar and flour with whisk until well blended. Gradually beat into chocolate mixture.

LINE 12 muffin pan cups with paper liners; spray with cooking spray. Place 1 cookie, upside-down, on bottom of each cup; cover with batter.

BAKE 8 min. or until cakes are firm around edges but still soft in centers. Cool in pan 1 min. Carefully remove cakes from pan. Invert into dessert dishes; remove paper liners. Serve with **COOL WHIP**.

MAKES: 1 doz. or 12 servings.

make ahead:

Batter can be prepared ahead of time. Cover and refrigerate up to 24 hours. When ready to serve, pour batter evenly over cookies in prepared muffin cups and bake as directed.

Nutrition Information Per Serving: 240 calories, 15g total fat, 9g saturated fat, 105mg sodium, 26g carbohydrate, 18g sugars, 3g protein.

OREO celebration cake

2 Tbsp. unsweetened cocoa powder

20 **OREO** Cookies, divided

1½ cups flour

1 tsp. **CALUMET** Baking Powder

1 tsp. baking soda

2 eggs, separated

1 cup granulated sugar

⅔ cup butter or margarine, softened, divided

1 cup water

½ cup **BREAKSTONE'S** or **KNUDSEN** Sour Cream

2 squares **BAKER'S** Semi-Sweet Chocolate, melted

2½ tsp. vanilla, divided

1 pkg. (16 oz.) powdered sugar, divided

3 Tbsp. milk

Chocolate Glaze (recipe follows)

HEAT oven to 350°F.

SPRAY 2 (9-inch) round pans with cooking spray; dust with cocoa powder. Coarsely chop 7 cookies. Finely crush remaining cookies; place in medium bowl. Add flour, baking powder and soda; mix well.

BEAT egg whites with mixer on high speed until stiff peaks form; set aside. Beat granulated sugar, ⅓ cup butter and egg yolks with mixer until well blended. Add flour mixture, water, sour cream, melted chocolate and 1 tsp. vanilla; beat on medium speed 1 min. Gently stir in egg whites until well blended. Pour into prepared pans.

BAKE 25 min. or until toothpick inserted in centers comes out clean. Cool in pans 10 min. Remove to wire racks; cool completely.

BEAT 1 cup powdered sugar with remaining butter and vanilla in large bowl with mixer until well blended. Add remaining powdered sugar alternately with milk, beating well after each addition. Reserve ½ cup frosting.

PLACE 1 cake layer on plate; spread with remaining frosting. Sprinkle with chopped cookies; top with remaining cake layer. Spread top with Chocolate Glaze. Let stand 10 min. Decorate with reserved frosting. Keep refrigerated.

MAKES: 16 servings.

Nutrition Information Per Serving: 410 calories, 17g total fat, 9g saturated fat, 260mg sodium, 67g carbohydrate, 49g sugars, 4g protein.

48

PREP TIME: **25** MINUTES

CHOCOLATE GLAZE

PREP: 5 min. TOTAL: 10 min.

- 4 squares **BAKER'S** Semi-Sweet Chocolate
- 1 Tbsp. butter or margarine

MICROWAVE chocolate and butter in microwaveable bowl on HiGH 1 min. or until chocolate is melted and mixture is well blended, stirring every 30 sec.

MAKES: 1/2 cup or 8 servings, 1 Tbsp. each.

Nutrition Information Per Serving: 80 calories, 6g total fat, 3.5g saturated fat, 10mg sodium, 8g carbohydrate, 6g sugars, less than 1g protein.

eggnog eclair dessert

- 1 pkg. (8 oz.) **PHILADELPHIA** Cream Cheese, softened
- 2 cups cold milk
- 1 pkg. (3.4 oz.) **JELL-O** Vanilla Flavor Instant Pudding
- 1/2 tsp. rum extract
- 1/4 tsp. ground nutmeg
- 1 tub (8 oz.) **COOL WHIP** Whipped Topping, thawed, divided
- 78 **NILLA** Wafers
- 2 squares **BAKER'S** Semi-Sweet Chocolate

BEAT cream cheese in large bowl with mixer until creamy. Gradually beat in milk. Add dry pudding mix, extract and nutmeg; beat 2 min. Gently stir in 1 1/2 cups **COOL WHIP**.

LINE 9×5-inch loaf pan with plastic wrap. Arrange 15 wafers, top-sides down, on bottom of pan; cover with 1/4 of the pudding mixture. Repeat layers 3 times. Top with 15 of the remaining wafers. Refrigerate 3 hours.

INVERT dessert onto plate; remove plastic wrap. Microwave chocolate and 1 cup of the remaining **COOL WHIP** in microwaveable bowl on HIGH 25 sec.; stir until chocolate is completely melted and mixture is well blended. Cool 1 min. Pour over dessert. Garnish with remaining **COOL WHIP** and wafers.

MAKES: 12 servings.

variation:
Omit rum extract and substitute eggnog for the milk.

Nutrition Information Per Serving: 300 calories, 17g total fat, 10g saturated fat, 300mg sodium, 35g carbohydrate, 23g sugars, 4g protein.

PREP TIME: 30 MINUTES

tiramisu bowl: serve it your way!

- 1 pkg. (8 oz.) **PHILADELPHIA** Cream Cheese, softened
- 3 cups cold milk
- 2 pkg. (3.4 oz. each) **JELL-O** Vanilla Flavor Instant Pudding
- 1 tub (8 oz.) **COOL WHIP** Whipped Topping, thawed, divided
- 48 **NILLA** Wafers
- 1/2 cup brewed strong **MAXWELL HOUSE** Coffee, cooled
- 2 squares **BAKER'S** Semi-Sweet Chocolate, coarsely grated
- 1 cup fresh raspberries

FOR THE FILLING:

BEAT cream cheese in large bowl with mixer until creamy. Gradually beat in milk and dry pudding mixes. Gently stir in 2 cups **COOL WHIP**.

NOW, YOU CHOOSE!

BOWL: Line bottom and side of 2 1/2-qt. bowl with half the wafers; drizzle with half the coffee. Top with half the pudding mixture and chocolate. Repeat layers. Top with remaining **COOL WHIP** and raspberries. Refrigerate 3 hours.

PAN: Line bottom of 13×9-inch pan with half the wafers; drizzle with half the coffee. Top with half the pudding mixture and chocolate. Repeat layers. Top with remaining **COOL WHIP** and raspberries. Refrigerate 3 hours.

PARFAITS: Place 1 wafer on bottom of each of 16 dessert dishes; drizzle each with 3/4 tsp. coffee. Top each with 1/4 cup pudding mixture and a sprinkle of chocolate. Add layers of remaining wafers and pudding; top with remaining chocolate, **COOL WHIP** and raspberries. Refrigerate 3 hours.

MAKES: 16 servings, about 2/3 cup each.

Nutrition Information Per Serving: 230 calories, 12g total fat, 7g saturated fat, 300mg sodium, 29g carbohydrate, 20g sugars, 3g protein.

ginger snap-apple mallow crisp

  6 Granny Smith apples (3 lb.), peeled, thinly sliced

  1 cup **JET-PUFFED** Miniature Marshmallows

18 **NABISCO** Ginger Snaps, finely crushed (about 1 cup)

1/2 cup chopped **PLANTERS** Pecans

1/4 cup butter or margarine, softened

  1 cup thawed **COOL WHIP** Whipped Topping

HEAT oven to 350°F.

PLACE apples in 8-inch square baking dish sprayed with cooking spray; top with marshmallows.

MIX ginger snap crumbs, nuts and butter until well blended; sprinkle over marshmallow layer.

BAKE 20 to 25 min. or until apples are tender. Serve topped with **COOL WHIP**.

MAKES: *9 servings, 1/2 cup each.*

note: ◄
Check dessert after the first 10 min. of the baking time. If it is becoming too brown, cover it loosely with foil for the rest of the baking time.

Nutrition Information Per Serving: 230 calories, 12g total fat, 5g saturated fat, 140mg sodium, 30g carbohydrate, 22g sugars, 2g protein.

PREP TIME: 15 MINUTES

CHIPS AHOY! sweetheart valentine's cookies

24 **CHIPS AHOY!** Cookies

4 squares **BAKER'S** Semi-Sweet Chocolate, melted

   Assorted decorations (colored sprinkles, colored sugars and assorted small candies)

   Decorating icings or gels

DIP bottoms of cookies in chocolate; place on waxed paper-covered baking sheets. Let stand until chocolate is firm.

ADD decorations, attaching to cookies with icings or remaining melted chocolate.

WRITE messages on cookies with icings.

MAKES: 2 doz. or 24 servings.

how to make a cookie bouquet:

Make your cookies into a bouquet of flowers by attaching a lollipop stick or wooden pop stick to the back of each cookie when coating in melted chocolate. Let stand until chocolate is firm. Decorate with assorted candies, sprinkles or colored sugars and decorating icings to resemble flowers. Tie 2 or 3 cookie flowers together with a ribbon. Wrap in cellophane for gift-giving.

Nutrition Information Per Serving: 90 calories, 4.5g total fat, 2g saturated fat, 45mg sodium, 14g carbohydrate, 9g sugars, less than 1g protein.

firecracker bites

1	pkg. (8 oz.) **PHILADELPHIA** Cream Cheese, softened
1	cup cold milk
1	pkg. (3.4 oz.) **JELL-O** Vanilla Flavor Instant Pudding
1½	cups thawed **COOL WHIP** Whipped Topping, divided
1	pkg. (12 oz.) **NILLA** Wafers
½	cup mixed red, white and blue sprinkles
42	pieces red string licorice (1 inch)

BEAT cream cheese in large bowl with mixer until creamy. Gradually beat in milk. Add dry pudding mix; beat 2 min. Whisk in 1 cup **COOL WHIP**.

SPOON about 1½ Tbsp. pudding mixture onto each of half of the wafers; cover with remaining wafers to make sandwiches. Freeze 2 hours or until filling is firm.

SPREAD tops of wafer sandwiches with remaining **COOL WHIP**. Dip in sprinkles. Insert licorice piece in top of each for the fuse. Freeze until ready to serve.

MAKES: 14 servings, 3 wafer sandwiches each.

variation:

Omit sprinkles. Divide ¾ cup BAKER'S ANGEL FLAKE Coconut into thirds. Place 2 portions in separate resealable plastic bags. Add 2 drops blue food coloring to coconut in one bag and 2 drops red food coloring to coconut in second bag. Seal bags; shake until coconut is evenly tinted. Prepare as above for sprinkles.

Nutrition Information Per Serving: 260 calories, 12g total fat, 6g saturated fat, 270mg sodium, 35g carbohydrate, 24g sugars, 3g protein.

OREO turkey

   6 **OREO** Cookies
   1 square **BAKER'S** Semi-Sweet Chocolate, melted
  30 pieces candy corn
   6 chocolate malted milk balls
   6 cinnamon red hot candies

SEPARATE each cookie, leaving all the cream filling on 1 half of each. Set filling-topped halves aside.

USE small amount of melted chocolate to attach 5 candy corn pieces, pointed-sides down, to each plain cookie half for the turkey's tail. Refrigerate 5 min. or until chocolate is firm.

ATTACH malted milk ball to center of each filling-topped cookie half with melted chocolate for the turkey's body. Use dot of melted chocolate to attach cinnamon candy to each body for the head.

ATTACH turkey tails to bodies with remaining melted chocolate. Refrigerate until firm.

MAKES: 6 servings.

how to easily separate cookies:

Refrigerate cookies for 15 min. before carefully twisting top from bottom so that the cream remains entirely on 1 half of the cookie. Use a knife to smooth filling if necessary.

Nutrition Information Per Serving: 150 calories, 6g total fat, 3g saturated fat, 85mg sodium, 24g carbohydrate, 18g sugars, 1g protein.